MW00785825

MAKING
POTTERY
WITHOUT A KILN

HAPPY LITTLE PROJECTS TO MAKE FOR YOUR HOME

DANIELA SCHMIDT-KOHL

Fox Chapel
PUBLISHING

Foreword

Crafting and I have a lifelong friendship. For as long as I can remember, I have been working with a variety of creative materials and techniques, but modeling clay has always been a constant companion.

Using your own hands to create art is so satisfying, and modeling clay is the perfect material to work with. With just a few tricks, you can make wonderful decorative items, accessories, and small gifts that look *almost* like real ceramics—all without a kiln!

I've included an entire year's worth of modeling clay projects. From spring-themed gift tags and summer wall decorations to autumnal bowls and wintery candleholders, there are useful projects for every season.

I've also explained how to best use modeling clay, what to watch out for when crafting, and techniques for creating different surface textures.

From quick, small projects to larger decorative items, I'll guide you step by step through each finished piece! Once you've worked your way through the projects in the book, you can find even more creative ideas on my Instagram: @klickerkram.

For now, I hope you have fun on your new creative adventure!

26

52

Contents

Materials   6
Tools   8

Projects for Spring   *12*

Windowsill Herb Markers   14
Bird Ornament   18
Upcycled Tin Can Flowerpot   22
Floral Relief Jewelry Dish   26
"Family, Love, Home" Tile Sign   30
"Home" Key Rack   34
Art Deco Relief Gift Tag   38

Projects for Summer   *42*

Flying Fish Ornament   44
Small Plant Relief Garland   48
Tropical Gift Tag   52
Air Plant Holder   56
Tiled Tray   60
Boho Chic Wall Mandala   66
Jam Jar Tag   70

Projects for Autumn   *74*

"Milk and Sugar" Coffee Tray   76
"Fall in Love" Bottle Tag   80
Forever Leaf Ornaments   84
Autumn Jewelry Dish   88
Framed Plant Print   92
Modern Circles Wall Decor   96
Woodland Plant Stakes   100

Projects for Winter   *104*

Houses Key Rack   106
Christmas Gift Tags   112
Tiled Wooden Box   116
Winter Ornaments   120
Place Card Candleholders   124
Personalized Napkin Rings   128
Simple Star Ornaments   132
Lucky Charm Gift Tags   136

Acknowledgments   142
About the Author   142
Index   143

Materials

The projects in this book are made with modeling clay and air-hardening clay. Each has different properties, so you should try working with each to discover which best suits your work. All the projects in this book can be made with either material, however, so you can work with the one you like best.

Objects made with modeling clay or air-hardening clay are not as durable as real ceramics, so keep that in mind when handling your finished pieces.

MODELING CLAY

Modeling clay is easy to shape and is very similar to polymer clay or ceramic clay. You can use it to create ceramic-like objects that can be painted and decorated with a wide variety of techniques. Modeling clay is also available in different colors.

For the projects in this book, I only used white modeling clay. Since it dries white, there is no need to paint your finished piece unless you want a different color.

Modeling clay tends to warp while drying, so you need to keep an eye on your piece and turn it occasionally during the drying process.

Modeling clay cannot be made workable again once it has dried.

AIR-HARDENING CLAY

Air-hardening clay is processed in a similar way to modeling clay. Air-hardening clay dries to a gray color, so unless you want a gray finish, you'll need to paint your pieces. I recommend using this as a design tool. For example, using white paint on pieces with embossed lettering creates a fantastic effect: the lettering stands out brilliantly against the gray tone.

Air-hardening clay also tends to bend less than modeling clay during the drying process, and it can even be repaired once it has hardened! Use slurry (clay softened in water that has a mud-like consistency) to reconnect any broken parts.

Air-hardening clay can be made workable again if it has dried out—just add water.

Both clays look the same in their packaging, but air-hardening clay dries gray while modeling clay stays the same color.

TIP

Make sure to put any extra clay away between projects! Otherwise, it will dry out and be wasted.

Along with the basic clay supplies, you can turn your project into an ornament or use them to decorate store-bought items.

Tools

BOWL OF WATER

The most important tools for working with modeling clay are your fingers and a bowl of water. You'll need moist hands to smooth the grooves and edges of your piece.

ROLLING PIN

Any rolling pin will work with clay, such as the classic wooden rolling pin. However, plastic or marble rolling pins are the best since they are smoother and will not add a rough texture to the modeling clay.

PARCHMENT PAPER

Parchment paper is a good base from which you can easily remove your modeling clay pieces.

POTTERY TOOLS

You can find special pottery tools in stores, such as a trimming tool or modeling tool. But household items like knives, spoons, wooden skewers, spatulas, toothpicks, etc., will work as well.

NEEDLES

You'll need a needle to remove air bubbles in rolled-out clay. Pierce the air bubble with the needle tip and gently press the air out, then use a moist finger to smooth out the modeling clay at the punctured spots.

SHARP, STRAIGHT KNIFE

A regular sharp knife works best to cut both modeling clay and air-hardening clay.

SQUARE WOODEN STICKS

Square wooden sticks will help you roll out the modeling clay to an even height. Place the sticks on either side of the clay to act as height spacers, then roll. I use wooden sticks that are ⅛" or ¼" (3 or 6mm) thick depending on the project. If you don't have square wooden sticks on hand, try using items like tiles or stacked wooden craft sticks.

SMALL STRAW

A small straw or hollow cake pop stick well help you make holes in your pieces. The hollow space in the straw punches out the modeling clay rather than displacing it, so your piece won't warp.

VERY FINE SANDPAPER

Use very fine sandpaper to smooth out rough spots after drying.

COOKIE CUTTERS

Cookie cutters of all kinds are useful tools. Use them to cut out base shapes for ornaments, tags, pendants, or bowls.

Rolling Pins

Square Wooden Sticks

Trimming Tool

Needle Tool

Thin Straws

Cookie cutters are great for making clay shapes, so start building up your collection!

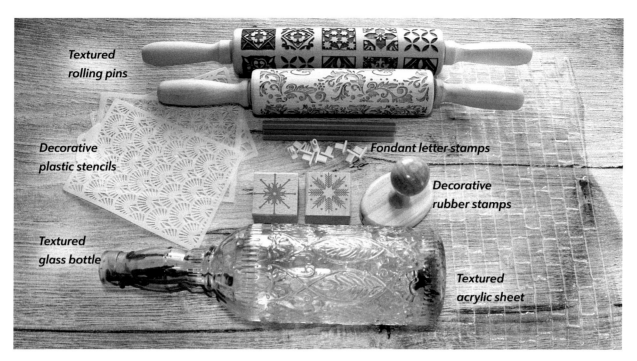

You can purchase acrylic and wooden texture tools, but you can also improvise with stamps, bottles, or anything else in your home.

Textured rolling pins

Decorative plastic stencils

Textured glass bottle

Fondant letter stamps

Decorative rubber stamps

Textured acrylic sheet

TEXTURE TOOLS

You can use many different craft and household objects to add texture to your pieces. Bottles with a textured exterior or plants from your garden might already be accessible.

A craft store is where you can find items like textured rolling pins, rubber stamps, and plastic stencils. These tools are also used for decorating baked goods and paper crafts, not just clay, so try exploring and see what you can find! You never know what will make a great texture in clay.

Depending on what tool you use, your design will be pressed into the clay or raised from the clay. The way you use these different textures will affect the design after drying.

PAINTS AND VARNISHES

After your piece has dried, you can decorate it with acrylic, craft, or chalk paints; lacquer pens; or even decoupage techniques. To achieve a ceramic-like look, I use high-gloss clear varnish (triple-gloss varnish). Alternatively, you can use epoxy or casting resin, just **be sure to follow the necessary safety precautions and manufacturer's instructions** when using it.

PAINTBRUSHES AND SPONGES

You will need paintbrushes or sponges to apply paint or varnish, depending on the decorating and finishing techniques you're using.

Use real leaves and other plant parts because all the intricate details will press into the clay.

Projects for Spring

WINDOWSILL
Herb Markers

Do you love having your own little herb garden on the windowsill as much as I do? If you're growing your own herbs, these markers are useful and pretty accessories—none of your plants will get mixed up after you make these!

YOU WILL NEED:

* Air-hardening clay
* Parchment paper
* ¼" (6mm) square wooden sticks
* Rolling pin
* Bowl of water
* Flag template (see above)
* Sharp knife
* Small straw or hollow cake pop stick
* Letter stamps

* 240 grit sandpaper, optional
* Sponge
* White acrylic paint
* Paintbrush
* High-gloss clear varnish
* Toothpicks or needle, optional
* 12 gauge (2mm) iron wire
* Wire cutters
* ½" (1.3cm) diameter wooden dowel or thick pencil, optional

········ TIP ········

If you plan to use your herb markers outside, make them with an oven-hardening clay (like polymer clay) or use clay sealant.

HOW TO DO IT:

1 Roll out the clay on parchment paper with a rolling pin. Place the square sticks to the left and right of the modeling clay. The rolling pin now rolls over the modeling clay and over the square wood at the same time! The height of the sticks therefore determines the height of the modeling clay.

2 Place the template on the clay, leaving enough room for all the flags you need. Cut out carefully using a knife.

3 Make a hole for the hook in each marker, using the straw or cake pop stick. Do not place too close to the edge.

4 Stamp the names of the desired herbs onto the flags. Learn more about the stamp tool on page 78. Smooth all edges with a finger moistened with water.

5 Leave the markers to dry. Sand if necessary, and paint using white paint and a sponge.

The sponge ensures that no brush strokes remain on the piece. Let the paint dry.

6 After the paint has dried, cover the markers with high-gloss clear varnish. For the most authentic ceramic look possible, use the varnish generously and smooth out any air bubbles that tend to form in the letters. If the bubbles cannot be removed with the brush, simply use a toothpick or needle to pierce them.

7 Cut three pieces of iron wire about 10" (25cm) long.

8 Bend hooks from the iron wire. Mold two loops to ensure the second is aiming the correct direction. A wooden dowel or a thick pencil can be helpful to use here.

9 Hang the markers on the hooks.

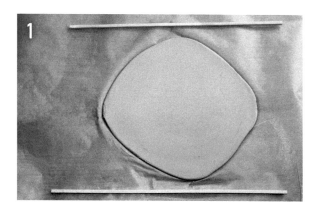

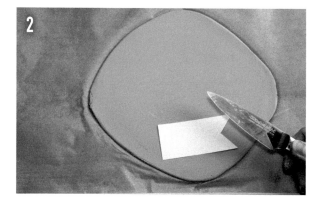

Bird Ornament

These cute little birds are the perfect spring decorations. You can hang them on a branch, use them as gift tags, or even as Easter decorations.

YOU WILL NEED:

* Modeling clay
* Parchment paper
* ⅛" (3mm) square wooden sticks
* Rolling pin
* Bowl of water
* Bird-shaped cookie cutter or template (see page 20)
* Thin cardboard, optional

* Small straw or hollow cake pop stick
* Napkin with floral motif
* Scissors
* Decoupage glue
* Paint brush
* High-gloss clear varnish
* Toothpicks, optional

HOW TO DO IT:

1 Roll out the clay on parchment paper with a rolling pin until it is evenly thick. Use the height of the square sticks for reference.

2 If using templates, trace the bird shape onto thin cardboard and cut out. Cut out birds from the modeling clay using a cookie cutter or a knife tracing the cardboard template. Smooth the edges with a moistened finger.

3 Use the straw or cake pop stick to make a hole in all ornaments for hanging. Do not place too close to the edge. Allow to dry thoroughly.

4 Cut out pretty pieces from the floral napkin. Separate the top layer of the napkin, the one with the motif, from the rest of the napkin layers.

5 Apply decoupage glue to the bird ornament with a paintbrush. Place the napkin piece on top, and gently smooth it out with the paintbrush and more glue. Leave to dry.

6 After drying, apply high-gloss clear varnish to the ornaments. Do not use too little varnish, or else you may not achieve the most beautiful ceramic look possible. Make sure the holes for a string do not become clogged. To remove any varnish, you can use a toothpick.

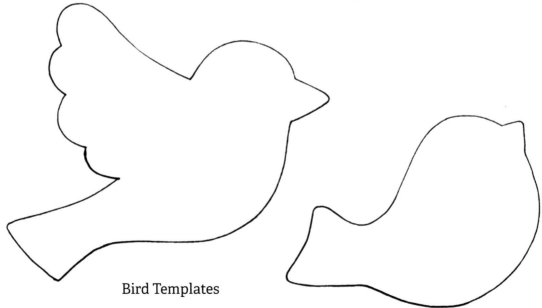

Bird Templates

TIP

If the napkin piece is wrinkled, you can put a little glue on your finger and carefully run it over the motif. This allows you to smooth out some wrinkles.

UPCYCLED TIN CAN
Flowerpot

Sometimes your decorations need a breath of fresh air. Especially in spring!
New plant pots are the perfect way to do it. You can even make your very
own unique piece from empty tin cans covered with embossed modeling clay.

YOU WILL NEED:

* Modeling clay
* Parchment paper
* ¼" (6mm) square wooden sticks
* Rolling pin
* Bowl of water
* Small tin can
* Tape measure or ruler
* Bottle with relief texture or another embossing tool

* Sharp knife
* Modeling tool with a tip
* Sponge
* Acrylic, chalk, or craft paint
* Paintbrush
* Matte clear-coat varnish, optional

HOW TO DO IT:

1 Measure the circumference and height of the can, then add about ¾" (2cm) to the length and about ⅓" (1cm) to the width. Roll the clay on parchment paper to the extended dimensions of the can or longer if possible. Ensure the clay is evenly thick, using the height of the square sticks for reference. Add a pattern to the modeling clay using the embossing tool you have chosen.

2 Measure the extended length and width on the modeling clay. The square wooden sticks can be used as markers.

3 Cut the modeling clay to the appropriate size. You are still using the extended dimensions from step 1.

4 Place the modeling clay around the can. Make sure that the band is not too tight, as it will shrink when drying. Cut off the excess end of the clay.

5 Score (roughen slightly using a modeling tool) the two open edges so that they can be connected more easily.

6 Join the edges together. Press the clay so the edges meld; they will not stay together if there is a distinct seam in the clay. Smooth out the seam and any uneven areas with a moistened finger. Leave the flowerpot to dry. If the seam tears while drying, you can simply close it again with some modeling clay.

7 Use a paintbrush to dab paint into the recesses of the piece, and immediately wipe the flowerpot with the damp sponge, applying only a little pressure. This leaves the color in the recesses and creates a wonderful vintage look. Paint in small areas to make sure the paint does not have too much time to dry. To make the flowerpot appear more durable, it can also be given a matte clear varnish.

ROLLING ON A TEXTURE

When using a textured rolling pin, a bottle with textured exterior, or another similar tool, you want to press the pattern in one pass. It is extremely difficult to match the pattern perfectly on a second pass, which would cause a distorted image. Instead, take your time when rolling. Maintain even pressure as you go; keep it hard enough that you are making an impression but not too hard that you flatten the clay.

If needed, roll out the clay thicker than the desired height, then roll the textured tool with extra pressure.

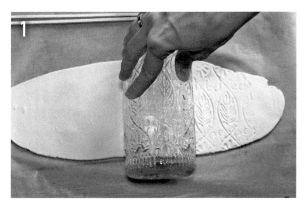

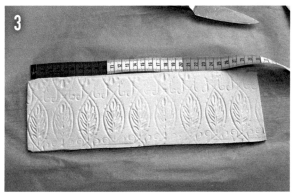

FLORAL RELIEF

Jewelry Dish

Bowls and dishes are wonderful decorative items that can be customized using clay. They are ideal for storing jewelry or keys.

YOU WILL NEED:

* Air-hardening clay
* Parchment paper
* ¼" (6mm) square wooden sticks
* Rolling pin
* Textured rolling pin
* Bowl of water
* Large circle cookie cutter, small plate, or bowl, optional

* Sharp knife
* Foam padding
* Acrylic dome
* Sponge
* White and green acrylic paint

1 Roll out the clay on parchment paper with a rolling pin until it is evenly thick. Use the height of the square sticks for reference.

2 Roll the textured rolling pin over the clay. Learn more about using a textured rolling pin on page 24.

3 Cut out a circle from the clay or use a plate or bowl as a template to cut out a circle. Smooth the edges with a finger moistened with water.

4 Place the circle on the foam padding with the pattern facing up. Place the curved side of the acrylic dome on the clay circle, and gently press the clay into the foam. Rotate the acrylic dome slightly, allowing the clay to raise on all edges.

5 Turn the dome upside down so the clay is laying on top. Gravity will help keep the shape. Let the clay bowl dry on the acrylic dome. Once dry, carefully remove the bowl from the dome; you may need to insert a thin item to help it pop off.

6 Using white, paint the entire bowl with a sponge.

7 Take a very small amount of green acrylic paint with the sponge. Carefully and with little pressure, go over the reliefs on the bowl. The paint should remain only on the raised parts of the pattern.

Foam Padding

This material is typically used for upholstery, whether making a new cushion or replacing an old one on a chair, bench, or other furniture item. They come in many sizes and thicknesses, depending on what you need. However, this can make for a soft surface that protects the base of your clay items while pressing into them.

If you do not want to invest money in foam padding just for this project, then try using something thick that you don't mind soiling with clay, such as a soft towel, scrap fabric, or old clothes that have been folded.

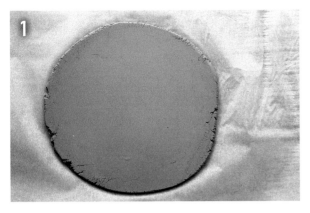

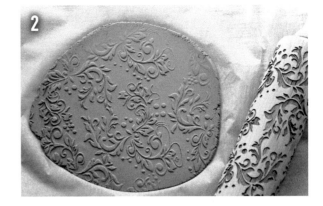

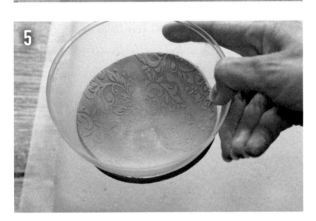

TIP

To give your jewelry dish more stability, you can place it on a small wooden ring as a base.

"FAMILY, LOVE, HOME"
Tile Sign

Feel like a new picture? This decorative sign with mini tiles is a beautiful eye-catcher and can be customized for your family. It is also a great gift for good friends.

YOU WILL NEED:

* Modeling clay
* Parchment paper
* ⅛" (3mm) square wooden sticks
* Rolling pin
* Bowl of water
* ¾" (2cm) craft foam letters
* 1¼" x 1¼" (3 x 3cm) square cookie cutter
* Needle tool or pin
* Paintbrush
* High-gloss clear varnish
* Construction adhesive
* 8½" x 11" (22 x 28cm) wooden board

1. Roll out the clay on parchment paper with a rolling pin until it is evenly thick. Use the height of the square sticks for reference.

2. Distribute the letters required for "family, love, home" or another phrase of your choice. Leave space between them on the modeling clay. Roll over them again with the rolling pin. Try to roll it out so the letters are level with the clay; however, this depends on the thickness of your letters.

3. Cut out all the letters using the cookie cutter. Keep the letters centered and upright. Be mindful of the surrounding letters.

4. Carefully remove the foam letters using a needle tool or pin. Poke the needle in enough to catch the foam, but not so far as to pierce the clay below. Gently rock the letter in place if it doesn't come loose easily.

5. Smooth all edges with a moistened finger. Allow the tiles to dry. Make sure that they do not bend while drying, and flip them if necessary.

6. Brush all the tiles generously with high-gloss clear varnish and leave to dry.

7. Plan out the correct arrangement of the tiles on the board. Leave about ¼" (6mm) gap between the letters. Glue using construction adhesive. Make sure to follow the manufacturer's instructions.

Another way to display this sign is to place it in a frame. I used a black frame here to make the tiles stand out even more.

"HOME"
Key Rack

With this key rack on the wall, you are guaranteed to never lose your keys again! And it looks pretty as a bonus.

YOU WILL NEED:

- ❄ Modeling clay
- ❄ Parchment paper
- ❄ ¼" (6mm) square wooden sticks
- ❄ Rolling pin
- ❄ Bowl of water
- ❄ 2½" x 2½" (6 x 6cm) square cookie cutter
- ❄ 1½" (4cm) letter stencils
- ❄ Sponge

- ❄ Black acrylic paint
- ❄ Paintbrush
- ❄ High-gloss clear varnish
- ❄ Construction adhesive
- ❄ 4" x 12" (10 x 30cm) wooden sign and picture-hanging hardware
- ❄ (4) ¾" (2cm) mini hooks and screws
- ❄ Electric or hand drill, optional
- ❄ Screwdriver

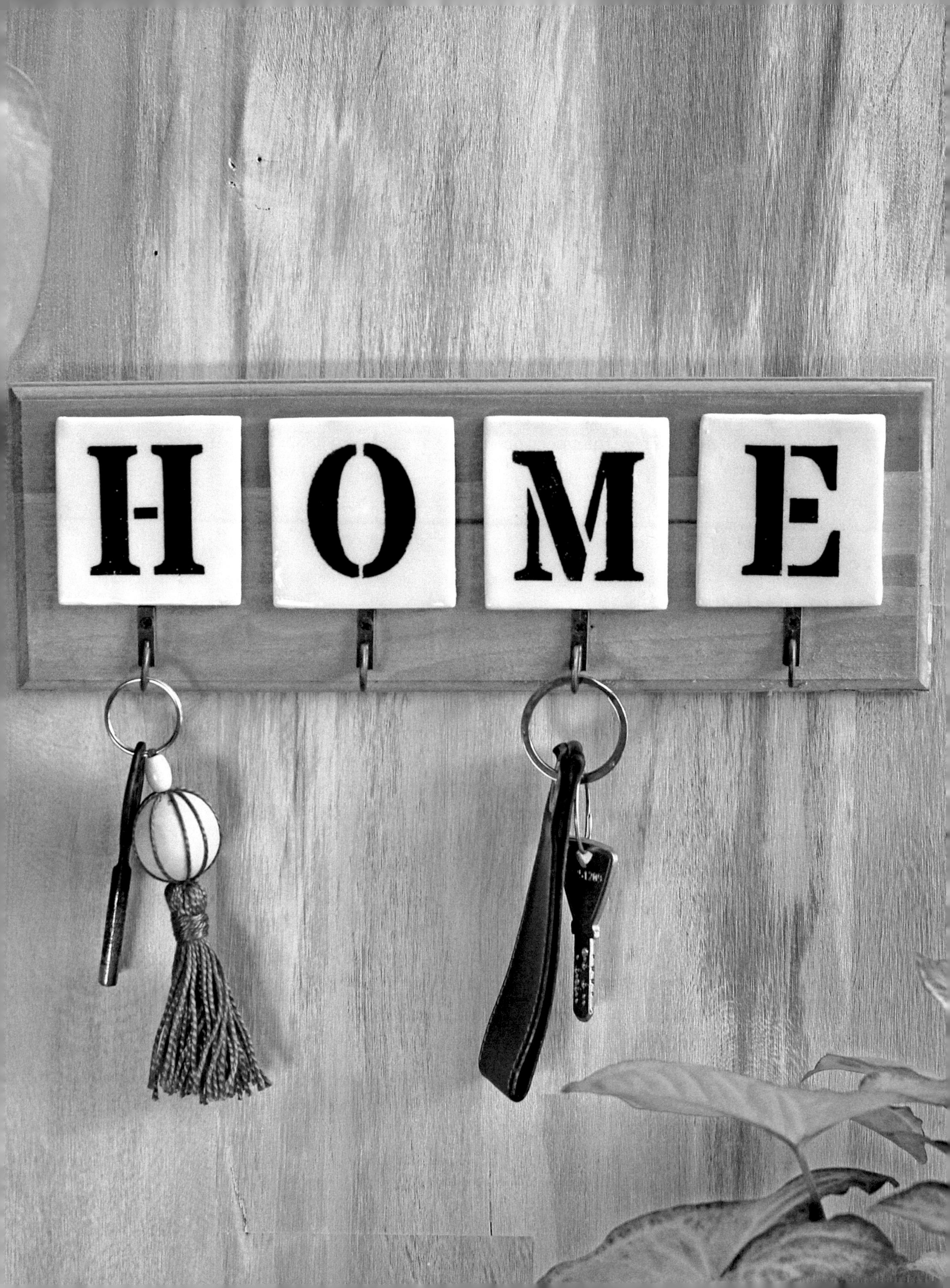
HOME

HOW TO DO IT:

1 Roll out the clay on parchment paper with a rolling pin until it is evenly thick. Use the height of the square sticks for reference.

2 Use the cookie cutter to cut out four tiles and let them dry.

3 Using a stencil, sponge, and black acrylic paint, apply one letter of the word "home" to each tile. Do not overdo it, less the paint travel under the stencil and ruin the clean look of the letter. Make sure the stencil does not slip. Allow to dry.

4 Generously brush the tiles with high-gloss clear varnish and leave to dry.

5 Arrange the tiles on the board ahead of glueing them. Leave about ¼" (0.6cm) gap between the letters and ½" (1.2cm) on either end. Attach the tiles to the wooden sign using construction adhesive, making sure to leave space for the hooks.

6 Mark the locations where the hooks are to be mounted. You may need to predrill the holes with a hand or electric drill to prevent the wood from cracking later.

7 Center all hooks under the tiles and fasten using the screwdriver.

WOOD COLOR

If you don't like the color of the wooden sign, you can change it! Here are some things to keep in mind:

1 Staining is the most common method for adjusting the color of your wood. This allows the woodgrain to show through while keeping a natural wood color. There are tons of stains out there all with pros and cons, such as drying times and how long they hold color. Do some research to see what works for you.

2 After staining, you will need to finish the wood. This can be with oil, varnish, shellac, or many other options. This may also depend on your staining technique.

3 If your wood is already finished, you will need to strip it away before staining again. However, a gel stain can be used on top of finished wood.

4 Paint is another fun option. It covers the woodgrain, but you can choose any color you like. Paint can be applied on top of a finish, though you should apply primer first and a topcoat after.

5 No matter what method you decide, always work in a well-ventilated area and follow the manufacturer's instructions.

ART DECO RELIEF
Gift Tag

If you love wrapping presents and gifts as much as I do, then these tags are a nice detail that you can use to add a special touch to any package.

YOU WILL NEED:

* Modeling clay
* Parchment paper
* ⅛" (3mm) square wooden sticks
* Rolling pin
* Bowl of water
* Oval-shaped cookie cutter
* Small straw or hollow cake pop stick
* Stencil with pattern

* Spatula
* Texture paste
* Green and gray acrylic or chalk paint
* Sponge
* Paintbrush
* High-gloss clear varnish
* Toothpicks, optional

1   Roll out the clay on parchment paper with a rolling pin until it is evenly thick. Use the height of the square sticks for reference.

2   Use the cookie cutter to cut out the tags from the modeling clay. Use the straw or cake pop stick to cut holes for ribbon, string, or twine. Do not place too close to the edge. Smooth all edges with a finger moistened with water and leave the tags to dry.

3   Place the stencil on a tag. Use a spatula to spread texture paste onto the stencil. Place the paste down and pull with your spatula, scraping the top for an even surface. You don't need a lot to achieve a relief. Make sure that the template does not slip.

4   Make sure the entire surface is covered before carefully peeling off the stencil. Clean the hole if needed. Let the texture paste dry.

5   Pick up a **little** paint at a time with the sponge and carefully brush over the tag. This means that the paint remains predominantly on the raised relief. Leave to dry.

6   Apply high-gloss clear varnish to the tags. Make sure that the holes do not become clogged. A toothpick, for example, can be used to remove varnish from the holes.

Plastic Stencils

Decorative plastic stencils are primarily used for paper craft projects, but they are a hidden gem for clay! There are all kinds of shapes, sizes, and patterns on the market. Most depict a particular image, like a flower or butterfly, that allows you to transfer that singular design onto paper or clay. However, I particularly enjoy the sheets that provide an allover decorative pattern. They act as a shortcut to carving your own pattern into clay. Learn more tips on how to use these stencils on page 102.

Projects for Summer

FLYING FISH
Ornament

With these ceramic-looking fish, you can bring summer to your living room. A small decorative lantern is also a wonderful gift for a summer party or a pretty table centerpiece.

YOU WILL NEED:

* Modeling clay
* Parchment paper
* ⅛" (3mm) square wooden sticks
* Rolling pin
* Bowl of water
* Fish-shaped cookie cutter
* Small straw or hollow cake pop stick

* Napkin with water design
* Scissors
* Decoupage glue
* Paintbrush
* High-gloss clear varnish
* Toothpicks, optional

1 Roll out the clay on parchment paper with a rolling pin until it is evenly thick. Use the height of the square sticks for reference.

2 Use the cookie cutter to cut out as many fish as you like.

3 Use the straw or cake pop stick to make a hole in each fish. Do not place too close to the edge. Smooth all edges with a moistened finger. Leave the ornaments to dry and flip them occasionally if they bend.

4 Cut out the appropriate number of fish bodies from the napkin; the cookie cutter can be used as a template. Then separate the top layer of the napkin from the rest.

5 Apply decoupage glue to each ornament and place a cut piece of napkin on top. Smooth the napkin with more decoupage. If there is any excess napkin, brush the decoupage around the edges to glue the extra down. Leave to dry.

6 Apply high-gloss clear varnish to the ornaments. Make sure that the holes do not become clogged. A toothpick, for example, can be used to remove varnish from the holes.

DECOUPAGE OPTIONS

Throughout this book, I use napkins as the decorative element for decoupage. This is mostly because the technique is paired with delicate ornaments, so the thin, tissue-paper quality looks best (in my opinion). However, there are plenty of other materials out there that you can use with decoupage!

Popular materials are decorative papers (such as for scrapbooks), book pages, magazine images, photographs, scrapbook papers, wallpaper, and even fabric. These all have different thicknesses and qualities to love. You may want to experiment to see what you like and how different these projects look when using another material.

SMALL PLANT RELIEF
Garland

Leaves and other parts of plants can be used to create and immortalize beautiful, intricate imprints. Strung together as a garland, they are sure to find a beautiful spot and spread their natural charm.

YOU WILL NEED:

* Air-hardening clay
* Parchment paper
* ⅛" (3mm) square wooden sticks
* Rolling pin
* Bowl of water
* Smaller plant parts
* Needle tool or tweezers

* 2" (5cm) diameter circle cookie cutter
* Small straw or hollow cake pop stick
* Sponge
* White, green, and gray acrylic paint
* Very fine and medium paintbrushes
* High-gloss clear varnish
* Toothpicks, optional

1 Roll out the clay on parchment paper with a rolling pin until it is evenly thick. Use the height of the square sticks for reference. Place the plant parts on top with some space between them.

2 Roll the rolling pin over the clay again so that the plants are pressed into the clay.

3 Remove all plant parts using a needle tool or tweezers. Do not place too close to the edge. Carefully go under the plant and lift. If there isn't a stem sticking out to allow an easy lift, poke and prod in an area that you know will not be part of your clay piece. This is usually the base but could be from a side that didn't turn out well and you will not include in your cut.

4 Use the circle cookie cutter to cut out pendants as desired. Use the straw or cake pop stick to make a hole in the pendant for hanging. Smooth all edges with a finger moistened with water and leave the pendants to dry.

5 Using white, paint the pendants with a sponge.

6 Mix different shades of green from the acrylic paints by using varying amounts of gray paint. Dilute the paints with water so they flow well. Using a very fine paintbrush, trace the main structures of the pressed plant shapes with the colored water. Try to let the color run into the thinner sections. This creates a very natural look, and the reliefs remain clearly visible. Leave to dry.

7 Generously coat the pendants with high-gloss clear varnish using the medium paintbrush. Make sure that the holes do not become clogged. A toothpick can be used to remove varnish from the holes.

SELECTING PLANTS

Sometimes, you gather materials for a project with super-high expectations, imagining it will turn out exactly like you have in your mind. And then reality comes crashing in when you make it. This is a bit of a dramatization of how I felt with one of the leafy greens I chose for this project. As you can see, the top-left plant doesn't make it into the final piece. This is because, when I rolled the plant into clay, it impressed far deeper than I wanted, looking a bit messy.

So here is wisdom that I can impart: try choosing plants that are flat. The scrapped plant was just a bit too dense. The textures didn't translate to the clay, instead overlapping too much and making it hard to see the individual leaves and veins. However, if you like the way this looks, then don't let me stop you! This just was not the effect I was looking for in this project. You might have the perfect place for this relief.

TROPICAL

Gift Tag

Temporary tattoos are a great and easy way to decorate objects made out of modeling clay. These simple gift tags evoke the feeling of vacation thanks to the tropical plant and flower tattoos!

YOU WILL NEED:

* Modeling clay
* Parchment paper
* ⅛" (3mm) square wooden sticks
* Rolling pin
* Bowl of water
* Oval-shaped cookie cutters
* Small straw or hollow cake pop stick

* Temporary tattoos with floral designs
* Scissors
* Sponge
* Paintbrush
* High-gloss clear varnish
* Toothpicks, optional

HOW TO DO IT:

1 Roll out the clay on parchment paper with a rolling pin until it is evenly thick. Use the height of the square sticks for reference. Use the cookie cutters to cut out the tags. Smooth the edges using a finger moistened with water.

2 Use a straw or cake pop stick to poke holes in the tags for a ribbon, string, or twine. Do not place too close to the edge. Leave them to dry. Make sure that they do not bend while drying and flip them if necessary.

3 Cut out suitable designs from the temporary tattoos. I selected two different design options: a singular design that will be centered in one tag, and a larger print that extends beyond the tag's area. These have slightly different looks, but both are fun! Experiment to see what you like. Use the cookie cutters as a template if needed.

4 Place the tattoo designs face down on the clay. Moisten the back of the temporary tattoo with a sponge.

5 Carefully lift off the backing paper; the tattoo should have come away from the backing. If that is not quite the case, moisten the paper again with the sponge. Leave the tattoos to dry.

6 Apply a generous coat of high-gloss clear varnish to the tags. Make sure that the holes do not become clogged. A toothpick can be used to remove varnish from the holes.

CRAFTING WITH TEMPORARY TATTOOS

Temporary tattoos are another decorating material that you might not think would work on clay, but it totally does! You can use them on ceramic casting clay, ceramic objects, and oven-hardening modeling clay. In fact, they can be used on almost any surface. For example, they can be used on paper for scrapbooking, on drinking glasses for an event, or terracotta pots for plants.

But that's not all! I've seen people put temporary tattoos on fabric, rocks, shells, and leaves. How amazing is that?

No matter what surface you place your temporary tattoos on, they are even better when protected with a coat of clear varnish. That way, they won't fade due to water, wear, or time.

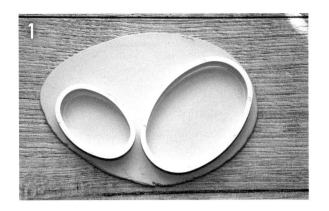

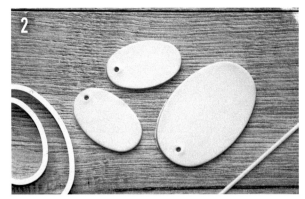

Air Plant

HOLDER

Air plants can be wonderfully decorated even in unusual places. This air plant holder provides a green accent on a wall.

YOU WILL NEED:

* Air-hardening clay
* Parchment paper
* ¼" (6mm) square wooden sticks
* Rolling pin
* Bowl of water
* Stencil with pattern
* 5½" x 3½" (14 x 9cm) oval-shaped cookie cutter
* Small and regular-sized straw or similar
* Sponge
* White and green acrylic paint
* Paintbrush
* High-gloss clear varnish

1 Roll out the clay on parchment paper with a rolling pin until it is evenly thick. Use the height of the square sticks for reference. Place the stencil on top.

2 Roll the rolling pin over the stencil without applying too much pressure, leaving an impression in the clay. Learn more about using plastic stencils on page 102.

3 Cut an oval out of the clay using the cookie cutter.

4 Use the small straw to make a hole for twine at the top. Do not place too close to the edge. Use the regular-sized straw to make two holes about 1¼" (3cm) apart, placing just off center within the oval. You may want to measure the air plant first to ensure it will sit in the middle. Remove the air plant holder from the cookie cutter and leave it to dry. Keep an eye on the piece while it is drying and flip if necessary if it bends.

5 Paint the holder using white paint and a sponge. Leave it to dry.

6 Use the flat side of the sponge to pick up a little green acrylic paint, and carefully go over the raised reliefs of the pattern. You don't want to press too hard or else the green will go into the white areas; you want contrast between the areas and colors.

7 Apply high-gloss clear varnish to the back of the air plant holder and leave it to dry. Then brush high-gloss clear varnish onto the front. Thanks to this sealing, the air plant can be easily misted later while on the holder.

8 Cut a length of twine twice the length you need for hanging. Fold it in half and run through the top hole. Tie a knot, doubling as much as desired. Cut another length of twine for holding the air plant. Run through both holes so each end is in front. Insert the air plant and tie the twine tight enough to hold it in place.

TIP

A stencil with a small-scale pattern without large gaps is ideal for this design technique. This makes it easier to color the raised structures with the sponge.

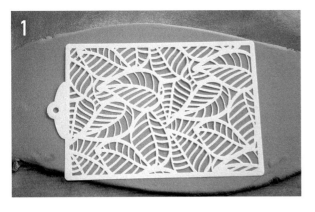

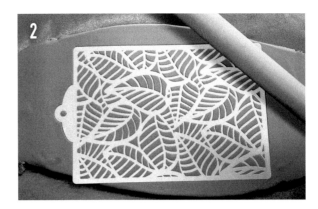

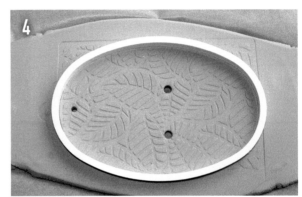

Tiled Tray

Trays are a practical accessory to decorate the center of a table, among many other options. It's easy to create a summery tray with matching homemade tiles.

YOU WILL NEED:

* Modeling clay
* Parchment paper
* ¼" (6mm) square wooden sticks
* Rolling pin
* Bowl of water
* Sharp knife
* Ruler
* Protractor
* (18) 2" x 2" (5 x 5cm) napkins with tile design

* Scissors
* Decoupage glue
* Paintbrush
* High-gloss clear varnish
* Construction adhesive
* 8" x 16" (20 x 41cm) wooden tray
* Chip brush
* Mosaic grout
* Sponge

HOW TO DO IT:

1 Roll out the clay on parchment paper with a rolling pin until it is evenly thick. Use the height of the square sticks for reference.

2 Use a knife and ruler to cut strips about 2" (5cm) wide into the modeling clay.

3 Use the protractor to determine a straight edge, and cut out 18 squares measuring approximately 2" x 2" (5 x 5cm). Smooth the edges using a finger moistened with water. Leave the tiles to dry. Make sure to flip them occasionally so that they do not bend on one side.

4 Cut out 18 squares from the napkins, centering on the mosaic design. Separate the top layer, the side with the design, from the remaining napkin layers.

5 Coat one tile at a time with decoupage glue, place a piece of napkin on top, and smooth it out with a paintbrush and more decoupage. Glue the excess over the edges. Continue in this way with all the tiles and leave to dry. Any wrinkles can be gently smoothed out with a finger moistened with glue.

6 Generously coat all the tiles with high-gloss clear varnish and leave to dry. →

CHECK THE SIZES

If you are using a tray with slightly different dimensions than 8" x 16" (20 x 41cm), you need to consider what else needs to change. A tray significantly smaller or larger may need more or fewer tiles. Another option is to change the size of the tiles to best fill the base. This change in tile size might also necessitate changing the number of tiles.

For a tray that is close in size to what is shown here, but not exact, you could adjust the spacing between tiles. Keep in mind that the gap between the tiles needs to be at least $\frac{1}{16}$" (1.5mm), though I would recommend more to ensure they stay in place.

All this requires a good amount of measuring and math. You may even want to sketch a diagram of the tiles and gaps to ensure you've accounted for everything. There's nothing worse than discovering your spacing is off at the end!

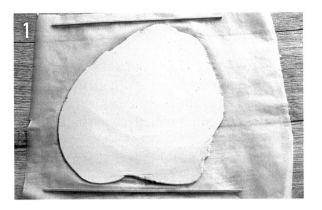
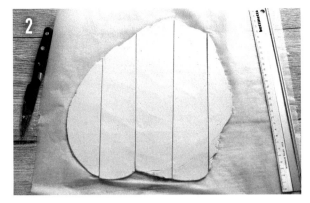
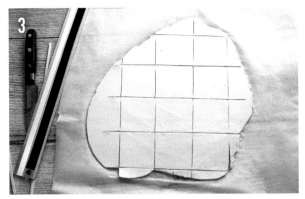

TIP

To make the wood of the tray a little more water-resistant, wax it before attaching the tiles. This way, the tray is less susceptible to stains in the grout from liquids you'll be carrying.

7 Arrange the tiles on the base ahead of glueing them. Leave about ½" (1.2cm) gaps between the tiles and the edges. Glue the tiles to the bottom of the tray using mounting adhesive. Make sure they are straight and even.

8 Mix the mosaic grout according to the instructions on the package. Spread it into the spaces between the tiles using a chip brush. Make sure there are no air holes. To do this, go over the gaps several times in different directions with the brush.

9 Allow the grout to set briefly, and then remove any excess grout with a damp sponge. Use a little pressure but not so much as to remove what should remain in the gaps.

10 Repeat this process until the tiles are reasonably clean. Leave to dry completely. Once completely dry, wipe off any remaining streaks with a damp cloth.

For ceramic tiles that look like this, you could easily pay a hundred dollars or more. This project is much cheaper and still easy!

Grout Color

When you buy grout, you'll likely see a whole lot of white and gray. But it doesn't need to stay that way! You can color your grout by adding acrylic paint to the mixture before applying to your tile. There are also powder pigments out there that you can add as well.

However, leaving your grout in a neutral color is a valid option. White provides a very clean look, while gray can help the colors in the tile stand out. Many mosaic artists prefer gray or black because it puts a spotlight on their work.

BOHO CHIC
Wall Mandala

Boho style is everywhere at the moment. With this wall mandala, you can easily bring unique flair into your home, onto your patio, or anywhere that needs a touch of nature.

YOU WILL NEED:

* Air-hardening clay
* Parchment paper
* ¼" (6mm) square wooden sticks
* Rolling pin
* Bowl of water
* Stencil with mandala pattern
* Large circle cookie cutter or small plate

* Small straw or hollow cake pop stick
* Sponge
* White and green acrylic paint
* Paintbrush
* Matte clear-coat varnish
* Toothpicks, optional

HOW TO DO IT:

1 Roll out the clay on parchment paper with a rolling pin until it is evenly thick. Use the height of the square sticks for reference. Place the template on the clay. Roll the rolling pin over the template with a little pressure so that it presses into the clay. Learn more about using plastic stencils on page 102.

2 Remove the template and use the cookie cutter to cut out a circle. Make sure that the relief is centered properly. Alternatively, use a small plate as a template, and cut out the clay all around with a knife.

3 Using a straw or cake pop stick, make a hole in the wall mandala for a ribbon, string, or twine. Do not place too close to the edge. Leave it to dry, paying attention to whether the piece bends and flipping if necessary.

4 Paint the mandala using white paint and a sponge. Leave to dry.

5 Paint the entire mandala green with a sponge or brush—do so quickly, so it is still wet for the next step. Pay particular attention to the gaps.

6 Immediately remove the paint from the raised parts with a damp sponge. To do this, wipe the relief with the flat side of the sponge without applying too much pressure. This creates a wonderful shabby look. Leave to dry.

7 Coat the mandala with matte varnish. Make sure that the hole for the string does not become clogged. If varnish does get stuck in it, a toothpick can be used to remove the excess.

MATTE VERSUS GLOSS

You're likely familiar with the term "gloss," but "matte" may be unfamiliar. These two are opposites when it comes to any kind of finish, whether it's on a car, your nail polish, or a craft project. Gloss makes the finished piece shine in the light, often emphasizing the areas in high relief. Matte, however, can make a piece look flat or dull. These terms are not meant to be negative—just look at how beautiful this mandala looks! A matte finish makes this piece look like it's made of stone or that it's an ancient piece of pottery. Matte has its place, and you might just fall in love with it!

Jam Jar
TAG

Gifts from the kitchen are a great way to share love. Homemade jams are the classic example. These gifts can be made even more beautiful and personal with tags in a matching design!

YOU WILL NEED:

* Modeling clay
* Parchment paper
* ⅛" (3mm) square wooden sticks
* Rolling pin
* Bowl of water
* 1½" (4cm) diameter circle cookie cutter
* Small straw or hollow cake pop stick

* Napkin with strawberry design, or fruit of your choice
* Scissors
* Decoupage glue
* Toothpick or needle, optional
* Paintbrush
* High-gloss clear varnish

HOW TO DO IT:

1 Roll out the clay on parchment paper with a rolling pin until it is evenly thick. Use the height of the square sticks for reference. Cut out several circles with the cookie cutter. Smooth all the edges with a finger moistened with water.

2 Make a hole in all the circles using the straw or cake pop stick. Do not place too close to the edge.

3 Cut out circles from the napkin. Make sure that the motifs fit well on the circle. Use the cookie cutter as a template if needed.

4 Separate the top layer with the design from the napkin. Cover the circle of clay with decoupage glue and attach the napkin. Coat the tag with another layer of decoupage and smooth out any wrinkles with a finger moistened with glue.

5 If the napkin is on top, use a toothpick or needle to pierce the hole for a ribbon, string, or twine. Leave to dry.

6 Apply a generous coat of high-gloss clear varnish to the tags. Make sure that the holes do not become clogged.

TIP

Always only use the top layer of the napkin that has the motif on it. This helps the design to remain wrinkle-free, and the applied napkin adapts better to the color of the surface, as it can show through a little.

Projects for Autumn

"MILK AND SUGAR"

Coffee Tray

Sitting down for coffee and tea has never been so inviting. Milk and sugar have the perfect place at the table with this small tray, which can be conveniently carried back and forth.

YOU WILL NEED:

- Modeling clay
- Parchment paper
- ⅛" (3mm) square wooden sticks
- Rolling pin
- Bowl of water
- Letter stamps
- Thin cardboard
- Scissors or box cutter
- Ruler
- Sharp knife

- Small straw or hollow cake pop stick
- Paintbrush
- High-gloss clear varnish
- 4" x 8" (10 x 20cm) tray, with ¾" (2cm) high edge
- Electric or hand drill, optional
- Small screws
- Screwdriver

MILK AND SUGAR

1 Roll out the clay on parchment paper with a rolling pin until it is evenly thick. Use the height of the square sticks for reference. Stamp the words "milk and sugar" into the clay.

2 Cut a rectangular template out of the cardboard, ensuring it fits generously over the lettering. Make sure to leave room for the screws on either side. Here, the template size is ½" x 4¾" (1.5 x 12cm). Place it over the stamped letters, and cut the label out of the modeling clay with a knife. Smooth all edges with a moistened finger.

3 Make a hole for the screws on the left and right of the letters using a straw or cake pop stick. Check the size of the holes against your screws, and expand the holes if needed.

Do not place too close to the edge. Leave to dry. It's especially important that the edges to not bend here or else the label will not lay flat or screw into place properly. Keep an eye on it and flip if necessary.

4 Coat the label with high-gloss clear varnish. Make sure that the holes do not become clogged. Leave to dry.

5 Place the label on the edge of the tray and mark the locations for the screws with a pointed object. If necessary, predrill the holes so that the wood does not crack.

6 Attach the label to the edge of the tray using the small screws.

Fondant Letter Stamp

I discovered this handy tool in the baking section of my local craft store. The kit comes with all the letters of the alphabet and an embosser that you can slide the letters onto. This way, you can make words, phrases, or names—anything can be customized using this handy tool! I also like these stamps over rubber stamps because this allows letters to sit closer together without the worry of accidentally overlapping them.

To use, stamp them straight down and lift to get a good impression. Do not press the stamp too deeply into the clay. Also, you do not need to move it back and forth; the edges of the stamp or embosser may show in the clay.

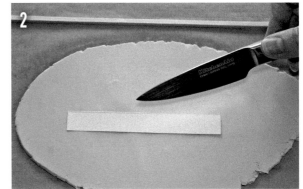

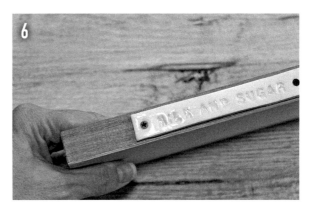

"FALL IN LOVE"
Bottle Tag

By adding a simple tag, you can quickly transform an apothecary bottle into a decorative autumn accessory. There are no limits to your imagination.

YOU WILL NEED:

* Air-hardening clay
* Parchment paper
* ⅛" (3mm) square wooden sticks
* Rolling pin
* Bowl of water
* Letter stamps
* Stamp with leaf design
* 2¾" (7cm) diameter circle cookie cutter
* Small straw or hollow cake pop stick
* Apothecary bottle
* Sponge
* White acrylic paint
* Paintbrush
* High-gloss clear varnish

1   Roll out the clay on parchment paper with a rolling pin until it is evenly thick. Use the height of the square sticks for reference. Stamp the words "fall in love" or another phrase of your choice into the clay. Learn more about the stamp tool on page 78.

2   Stamp leaf designs around the lettering. Place the stamps as desired around the writing to create a visually appealing image. Silicone stamps are particularly suitable here.

3   Cut out the motif using the circle cookie cutter, keeping the words centered.

4   Using a straw or cake pop stick, make a hole for string on the left and right of the tag. Do not place too close to the edge. Smooth all edges with a moistened finger.

5   Place the tag on the bottle and bend it to match the curve. Leave to dry on the bottle. For a round bottle, you may need to prop up the sides to prevent it from rolling.

6   Paint the tag using white paint and a sponge. Leave to dry.

7   Coat the tag with high-gloss clear varnish. Make sure that the holes do not become clogged.

RUBBER STAMPS

I used silicone stamps for this project because they typically have a flat back. But you may have a collection of rubber stamps that would be perfect for this! When pressing into the clay, you may want to rock the stamp in place, moving in a circular direction. This ensures all the edges are made visible. However, do not press too hard or else it could distort the clay.

If desired, you could test your technique in a bit of extra clay before applying to your project.

FOREVER
Leaf Ornaments

These ornaments, which are made using real leaves, are perfect as an autumnal decorative accessory or as a gift tag.

YOU WILL NEED:

- Modeling clay
- Parchment paper
- ⅛" (3mm) square wooden sticks
- Rolling pin
- Bowl of water
- Natural leaves

- Sharp knife
- Tweezers or needle tool, optional
- Small straw or hollow cake pop stick
- Paintbrush
- High-gloss clear varnish

1 Roll out the clay on parchment paper with a rolling pin until it is evenly thick. Use the height of the square sticks for reference. Place the leaves with the veined side down on the modeling clay. Roll over the leaves and clay with the rolling pin. Do not press too hard; the leaves will not need much to leave an impression in the clay.

2 Cut out all around the leaves with a knife. Simplify the shape where necessary. For example, the green leaves had a slightly serrated edge, but I smoothed the sides to one smooth line.

3 Lift the leaves from the modeling clay. A needle tool or tweezers can be used here. Carefully pierce the leaf with the tool, trying if possible to not damage the modeling clay. Then lift the clay leaves from the surrounding modeling clay.

4 Smooth all edges with a moistened finger. Use the straw or cake pop stick to make a hole in each leaf for a ribbon, string, or twine. Do not place too close to the edge. Leave to dry.

5 Apply high-gloss clear varnish to the leaves. Make sure that the holes do not become clogged.

TIP

Look for leaves that have as many veins as possible on the back. They will give you dramatic, three-dimensional results! You could also use flowers or petals with this technique, as long as they have enough texture to transfer into the clay.

AUTUMN
Jewelry Dish

These small bowls bring autumn to the table! They are a wonderful storage spot for small items like necklaces, earrings, and rings.

YOU WILL NEED:

* Modeling clay
* Parchment paper
* ¼" (6mm) square wooden sticks
* Rolling pin
* Bowl of water
* Large circle cutter or small plate
* Sharp knife

* Foam padding
* Acrylic dome
* Napkin with autumn design
* Scissors
* Decoupage glue
* Paintbrush
* High-gloss clear varnish

1 Roll out the clay on parchment paper with a rolling pin until it is evenly thick. Use the height of the square sticks for reference.

2 Using a circle cutter, cut out a circle. You could also use a plate or bowl as a template. Smooth the edges with a moistened finger. Place the clay circle on the foam padding and press with the acrylic dome into the foam. Rotate the dome lightly over the modeling clay to ensure the edges are matching the curve. Turn the dome upside down so the clay is laying on top. Gravity will help keep the shape. Leave to dry on the acrylic dome.

3 Cut the designs out of the napkin close to the edge.

4 Separate the top layer with the motif from the rest of the napkin layers.

5 Coat the inside of the bowl with decoupage glue and place the motifs on top. Arrange the motifs harmoniously. You can also arrange these in advance without napkin glue to test what design you like. Cover the motifs again with decoupage, and gently smooth out any wrinkles with a finger moistened with glue. Leave to dry.

6 Coat the inside of the bowl with high-gloss clear varnish. Use a little less varnish here so that it does not pool too much into the center of the bowl.

TIP

Napkins with designs on a white background are best because you won't be able to see the edges of the motif on the finished piece. The design of the napkin practically merges with the bowl.

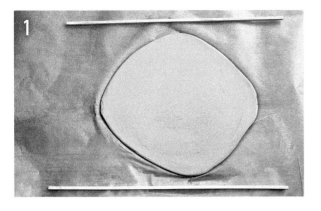

FRAMED
Plant Print

This picture, which is made with the help of real plants, is perfect to quickly bring a fresh breeze to your walls or picture rail while the leaves change outside!

YOU WILL NEED:

* Air-hardening clay
* Parchment paper
* ⅛" (3mm) square wooden sticks
* Rolling pin
* Bowl of water
* Leaves or other plant parts
* Thin cardboard
* Scissors or box cutter

* Needle or tweezers
* Metal ruler or sharp knife
* Sponge
* White and green acrylic paint
* Very fine and medium brushes
* High-gloss clear varnish
* Construction adhesive
* Decorative picture frames

1 Roll out the clay on parchment paper with a rolling pin until it is evenly thick. Use the height of the square sticks for reference. Place the plants on top, and roll over them and the clay with the rolling pin.

2 Cut a template out of the cardboard to the size you need. Here, the template was about ½" (1.3cm) smaller than the interior of the frame. Place the template on the clay and mark the edges. With the metal ruler or sharp knife, cut out the square. I flipped the clay upside down and cut from the back, but this isn't required.

3 Carefully peel the plants off the clay. Smooth all edges of the tile with a finger moistened with water. Leave to dry.

4 Paint the tile with white acrylic paint and a sponge.

5 Dilute the green acrylic paint so that it flows easily. Using a very fine brush, trace the main structures of the pressed plant with the colored water. Try to let the color run into the smaller areas. This creates a very natural look, and the reliefs remain clearly visible. Leave to dry.

6 Generously coat with high-gloss clear varnish using the medium brush.

7 Glue the tile into a frame using construction adhesive. Make sure it is centered.

Using Flowers

Flowers are another option for this project, whether you use a flower instead of a leaf or want to make multiple prints of the same style. Because there are so many options out there, you may need to experiment before deciding which flower is right for you. Something with too much texture may look messy while not enough may not produce a good relief.

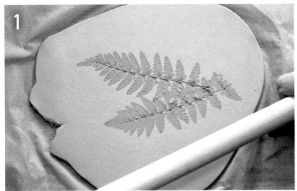

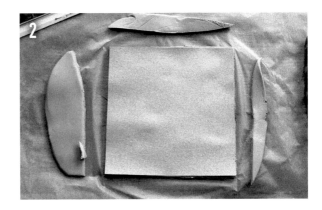

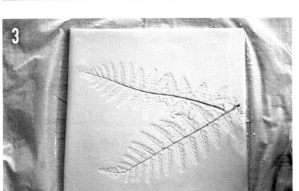

MODERN CIRCLES
Wall Decor

Thanks to the dipped elements, this simple wall decoration is a beautiful eye-catcher. If the front and back are designed the same, it can also be used as a free-hanging mobile.

YOU WILL NEED:

* Modeling clay
* Parchment paper
* ¼" (6mm) square wooden sticks
* Rolling pin
* Bowl of water
* 3 sizes of circle cookie cutters
* Small straw or hollow cake pop stick

* Painter's tape
* Sponge
* Gray acrylic paint
* Paintbrush
* High-gloss clear varnish
* Twine or nylon cord

HOW TO DO IT:

1 Roll out the clay on parchment paper with a rolling pin until it is evenly thick. Use the height of the square sticks for reference. Cut out three circles of different sizes.

2 Using the straw or cake pop stick, poke two holes (top and bottom) into the large and middle circles. Poke one hole (top) into the small circle. Do not place too close to the edge. Smooth the edges with a finger moistened with water. Leave the circles to dry. Pay attention to the pieces and flip them if necessary if they bend.

3 Use painter's tape to define a line on each of the three circles. Fully encase one half of the circle with tape, since you will be painting both sides.

4 Using the sponge, paint half of the circles gray. Paint first on one side, let dry, and then on the other side. Include the edges when you paint one of the sides. Leave to dry.

5 Remove the painter's tape. Generously coat the painted areas with high-gloss clear varnish.

6 Connect all three circles with twine or nylon cord. Cut a length of twine or cord twice the length you need for hanging. Fold it in half and run through the top hole. Tie a knot, doubling as much as desired.

> ⋯⋯ TIP ⋯⋯
>
> If you don't have circle cookie cutters on hand, or three of different sizes, you can also use different round objects as a template. Small plates, cups, or glasses are ideal here. You can simply place on the rolled-out modeling clay, then cut out all around it.

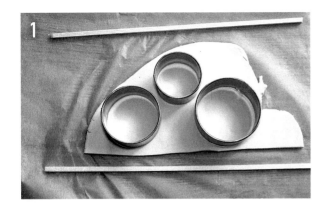

WOODLAND
Plant Stakes

Using cookie cutters, you can make beautiful stakes for your indoor plants. They can be used to enhance flower arrangements, flowerpots, or even gifts. These stakes could also be used as decorative plant markers!

YOU WILL NEED:

* Modeling clay
* Parchment paper
* ¼" (6mm) square wooden sticks
* Rolling pin
* Bowl of water

* Stencil with pattern
* Cookie cutters of your choice
* Thin wooden skewers
* Paintbrush
* High-gloss clear varnish

1 Roll out the clay on parchment paper with a rolling pin until it is evenly thick. It's important for this clay to be thick since you will be inserting skewers into the base. Use the height of the square sticks for reference. Place the stencil on the modeling clay and carefully roll over it again so that the pattern is imprinted.

2 Cut out shapes from the modeling clay using cookie cutters. Smooth all the edges with a finger moistened with water.

3 Carefully push a wooden skewer into the base of each cut-out shape. If the skewer is inserted at an angle, it will poke through the clay on one side. If the side is accidentally pierced, the hole can simply be closed again with a moistened finger.

4 Leave the stakes to dry. Keep an eye on the pieces, and flip them if necessary if they bend during drying. Generously cover the dried clay with high-gloss clear varnish.

IMPRINTING A TEXTURE

When using decorative plastic stencils, you must keep in mind how thin they are. While some pressure will be needed to properly transfer the design into clay, you do not need to press super hard to create texture in the clay.

Keep in mind that your rolling pin will flatten out the relief texture no matter what. Pressing too hard might just create unsightly areas that have lost their distinct design. Or, like with textured rolling pins, too much pressure may reduce the height of your clay.

It's better to go a bit too light than a bit too hard with this technique. After all, because these stencils lay flat on the surface, you can easily roll over the pattern again if needed.

TIP

When you push the wooden skewer into your clay, turn the skewer slightly. This will prevent the motif from warping too much.

Projects for Winter

HOUSES

Key Rack

Little houses are an absolute hit and an indispensable part of the decoration scene, especially in the cold season. This house key rack is not only pretty, but also a practical organizational aid.

YOU WILL NEED:

- ❋ House templates (see page 110)
- ❋ Thin cardboard
- ❋ Scissors or box cutter
- ❋ Modeling clay
- ❋ Parchment paper
- ❋ ⅛" (3mm) square wooden sticks
- ❋ Rolling pin
- ❋ Bowl of water
- ❋ Sharp knife
- ❋ Small square cookie cutter, optional

- ❋ 240 grit sandpaper, optional
- ❋ Paintbrush
- ❋ High-gloss clear varnish
- ❋ Picture-hanging hardware with screws
- ❋ Screwdriver
- ❋ 6¼" x 10" (16 x 25cm) wooden board
- ❋ Construction adhesive
- ❋ Electric or hand drill, optional
- ❋ (3) ¾" (2cm) small hooks

HOW TO DO IT:

1 Transfer the templates onto cardboard and cut them out. Roll out the clay on parchment paper with a rolling pin until it is evenly thick. Use the height of the square sticks for reference. Place the templates on the modeling clay.

2 Cut out all around the houses with a knife.

3 A small, square cookie cutter can be used for the windows. Or you can carefully cut out the windows according to the template with a knife. Don't pull the knife too hard or else the modeling clay may warp.

4 Smooth all edges with a finger moistened with water and leave the houses to dry Keep an eye on the pieces, and flip them if they bend.

5 Sand the edges of the houses if necessary. This can be to define any edges or remove unevenness. Apply a generous amount of high-gloss clear varnish.

6 Attach the picture-hanging hardware to the back of the board.

7 Orient the wooden board horizontally and the three houses vertically. Leave about ¼" (0.6cm) gap between the houses and ½" (1.2cm) on either end. Glue the houses onto the wooden board using construction adhesive, making sure that there is enough space below for the hooks.

8 Mark the locations where the hooks are to be mounted. If necessary, predrill the holes so that the wood does not crack.

9 Screw the hooks on tight.

House Templates

Customize the houses to look like your own residence for a personal touch!

CHRISTMAS
Gift Tag

Whether used as an ornament for the Christmas tree or a tag on a gift, these accessories are a real eye-catcher.

YOU WILL NEED:

* Modeling clay
* Parchment paper
* ⅛" (3mm) square wooden sticks
* Rolling pin
* Bowl of water
* Stamps with Christmas designs
* Oval or round cookie cutters

* Small straw or hollow cake pop stick
* Red and green acrylic paint
* Paintbrush
* Sponge
* High-gloss clear varnish
* Toothpicks or needle, optional

HOW TO DO IT:

1 Roll out the clay on parchment paper with a rolling pin until it is evenly thick. Use the height of the square sticks for reference. Apply designs with the stamps, leaving space between each as needed.

2 Cut out the designs using cookie cutters.

3 Use a straw or cake pop stick to poke a hole in each tag for a ribbon, string, or twine. Do not place too close to the edge. Smooth all edges with a finger moistened with water. Leave the tags to dry, flipping them over if necessary to prevent them from bending.

4 Prepare paint colors and an extra bowl of water. Dab one color at a time into the indentations of the relief with the brush.

5 Immediately wipe off the paint with the sponge. This creates a wonderful vintage look. The moisture causes the pendant to discolor slightly, but this goes away once it dries. Leave to dry.

6 After the paint has dried, coat the tags generously with high-gloss clear varnish. Make sure that no bubbles form. If bubbles appear, smooth them out with a brush, or use a toothpick or needle to puncture them

⋯⋯ DISCOLORED CLAY ⋯⋯

In step 5, I mention that the clay is discolored slightly. This is because the ornaments are not initially painted white. Since the modeling clay is in its raw state, when the paint is wiped off, it will change color due to the water. If you want to avoid this issue, paint the clay white, let it dry, and then paint the relief. However, you may want to lean into the mild discoloring of the clay. It's all up to you!

TILED
Wooden Box

This small wooden box can be used to store small items, like pens. With the right lining, it can also serve as a planter. Arranged with a small pine, it is a lovely decoration or gift in the run-up to the winter holidays.

YOU WILL NEED:

* Modeling clay
* Parchment paper
* ⅛" (3mm) square wooden sticks
* Rolling pin
* Textured rolling pin with tile design
* Bowl of water
* 1¼" x 1¼" (3 x 3cm) square cookie cutter or knife

* Green and gray acrylic paint
* Paintbrush
* Sponge
* High-gloss clear varnish
* Construction adhesive
* 3" x 2¾" (8 x 7cm) wooden box
* Chip brush
* Mosaic grout

1 Roll out the clay on parchment paper with a rolling pin until it is evenly thick. Use the height of the square sticks for reference.

2 Roll the textured rolling pin over the modeling clay to create a relief. Learn more about using a textured rolling pin on page 24.

3 Use the cookie cutter to cut out 16 tiles. Alternatively, cut the tiles to approximately 1¼" x 1¼" (3 x 3cm) with a knife. Smooth all edges with a finger moistened with water and leave the tiles to dry.

4 Prepare paint colors, brushes, sponges, and an extra bowl of water. Dab paint onto one tile.

5 Wipe the paint off the raised areas immediately with the sponge. This creates a wonderful vintage look. Continue to paint and wipe with the remaining tiles. Leave to dry.

6 Brush the tiles with high-gloss clear varnish and leave to dry. Glue them onto the wooden box using construction adhesive. Set the box on the base so you can access all four sides. Glue one side at a time. Leave to dry thoroughly.

7 Mix the mosaic grout according to the manufacturer's instructions. Spread the grout around the wooden box, on the joints, and in the gaps between the tiles with a chip brush. Allow to dry briefly.

8 After the short setting time, remove the grout from the surface with a sponge and water. Repeat this process until the tiles are almost clean. Be careful not to wipe the grout out of the gaps. The sponge should only be damp, not too wet, or else the grout may be rinsed out of the gaps. Let everything dry properly.

TIP

You can achieve a range of colors with just two paints. Adding more or less gray paint will affect the saturation, which is how bright or dull a color appears.

WINTER
Ornaments

Whether for decoration purposes or as gift tags, these winter-themed ornaments are sure to bring joy.

YOU WILL NEED:

* Air-hardening clay
* Parchment paper
* ⅛" (3mm) square wooden sticks
* Rolling pin
* Bowl of water
* Bauble-shaped cookie cutters
* Small straw or hollow cake pop stick
* Sponge

* White acrylic paint
* Gold acrylic paint or paint marker
* Napkins with winter plant patterns
* Scissors
* Decoupage glue
* Paintbrush
* High-gloss clear varnish

HOW TO DO IT:

1. Roll out the clay on parchment paper with a rolling pin until it is evenly thick. Use the height of the square sticks for reference.

2. Cut out the ornaments from the clay using bauble or circle cookie cutters. Use a straw or cake pop stick to make a hole in each one for a ribbon, string, or twine. Do not place too close to the edge. Smooth all the edges with a finger moistened with water. Leave to dry.

3. Paint the ornaments using a sponge and white paint.

4. Paint the cap of the baubles with the gold paint marker or gold acrylic paint. If making a circular ornament without a cap, draw a curve at the top and fill in with gold.

5. Cut out appropriate napkin pieces for the ornaments. Leave out the gold-painted parts. The cookie cutters can be used as a template. The cut does not have to be perfect, as the napkin adapts well to the surface.

6. Separate the top layer of the napkin, the one with the pattern, from the remaining layers.

7. Apply decoupage glue to the white areas of the ornaments and place the cut napkin on top. Smooth the napkin with more glue. If wrinkles form, they can be gently smoothed out with a finger moistened with glue. Leave to dry.

8. After the paint has dried, coat generously with high-gloss clear varnish.

TIP

If desired, you might find it easier to paint the ornament caps after applying the decoupage. This way, you can paint over the edge of the napkin with gold paint if it's not perfectly in place. Keep in mind that you will also be painting over the dried decoupage, rather than applying glue over the paint.

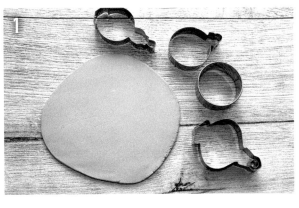

PLACE CARD
Candle Holder

A beautifully set table is a joy to behold, especially for the holidays. With these dual place cards and candle holders, guests also take home a small gift that they can enjoy again and again.

YOU WILL NEED:

* Modeling clay (preferably a new package)
* Parchment paper
* Rolling pin
* Bowl of water
* Star and pine tree cookie cutters
* Taper candles
* Letter stamps
* Paintbrush
* High-gloss clear varnish

HOW TO DO IT:

1 Roll out the modeling clay on the parchment paper to a height slightly shorter than the cookie cutters. A new package of modeling clay is ideal for this, as the freshly opened clay simply needs to be rolled out a little and is already nice and straight. Insert the cookie cutters into the modeling clay. Press one candle into the center of each motif; the depth should be about half the height of the modeling clay.

2 Release the molds when you have completely finished cutting. If you are reusing the cookie cutter, cut each one out of the large block before stamping the next one. Carefully press the clay out of the mold. Smooth the edges with a finger moistened with water.

3 Stamp the guests' names into the candle holder. Individual letter clay stamps or conventional small letter stamps can be used for this. Leave to dry.

4 Apply high-gloss clear varnish to the candle holder.

Using a different shape immediately makes these perfect for a wedding, a summer get-together, or any other occasion!

PERSONALIZED
Napkin Rings

With these pretty napkin rings, you can decorate the table for a special meal in no time—after all, you eat with your eyes too!

YOU WILL NEED:

* Modeling clay
* Parchment paper
* ⅛" (3mm) square wooden sticks
* Rolling pin
* Bowl of water
* Long cardboard tube

* Plastic wrap
* Thin cardboard
* Scissors or box cutter
* Sharp knife
* Letter stamps
* Modeling tool or knife

1 Roll out the clay on parchment paper with a rolling pin until it is evenly thick. Use the height of the square sticks for reference. Wrap the cardboard tube with plastic wrap.

2 Cut a 1½" x 6" (4 x 15.5cm) rectangular template out of the thin cardboard. Use the template to cut strips out of the modeling clay.

3 Stamp the strips with a phrase, a greeting, or the guest's name. Learn more about the stamp tool on page 78.

4 Place the strips around the prepared cardboard tube, facing the writing outward. If necessary, cut excess modeling clay close to the edge.

5 Score (roughen) the edges slightly with a modeling tool or knife. **Note:** Do not remove from the tube as shown. This was just to better show the edge.

6 Place edges together and join them using the modeling tool.

7 Smooth the edge with a finger moistened with water and the modeling tool. Allow the napkin rings to dry thoroughly on the kitchen roll. To remove the rings, the cardboard roll can be folded in slightly so that the napkin rings are no longer tight to the previous shape.

TIP

Look throughout this book for more inspiration on how to dress up napkin rings. For instance, you could decoupage a design onto the outside or press plants into the clay for an interesting relief. Alternatively, you could play with the shape. Rather than cutting out a straight rectangle, you could use a wave pattern or cut out a design from the center. There are so many possibilities!

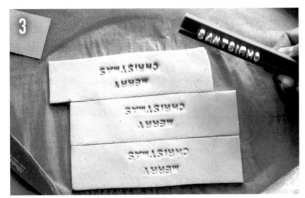

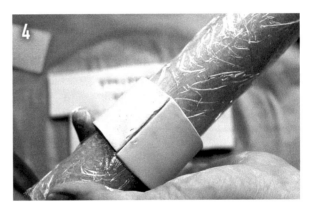

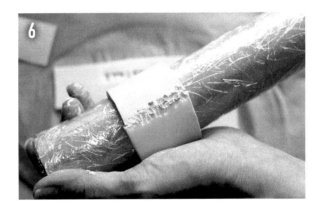

SIMPLE STAR
Ornaments

Stars are used in many winter holidays and the rest of the year. Made from modeling clay, they can be pretty gift tags, ornaments, or decorations for a lantern.

YOU WILL NEED:

* Modeling clay
* Parchment paper
* ⅛" (3mm) square wooden sticks
* Rolling pin
* Bowl of water
* Star cookie cutter
* Small straw or hollow cake pop stick

* Letter stamps, optional
* Paintbrush
* High-gloss clear varnish
* Toothpicks or needle, optional
* Ribbon, string, or twine

HOW TO DO IT:

1 Roll out the clay on parchment paper with a rolling pin until it is evenly thick. Use the height of the square sticks for reference. Cut out the stars with a cookie cutter.

2 Use a straw or cake pop stick to poke a hole in the stars. Do not place too close to the edge. Smooth out all the edges with a finger moistened with water.

3 If desired, stamp words or names into the clay. Learn more about the stamp tool on page 78. Let the stars dry. Keep an eye on the pieces, and flip them if they bend.

4 Apply a generous amount of high-gloss clear varnish. Make sure that no bubbles are left behind, which tend to form in the writing. Smooth out any bubbles with a brush, or use a toothpick or needle to pop them. Leave to dry.

5 Attach the ribbon, string, or twine to the stars.

While I made these for Christmas, your ornaments could easily be adapted for Hanukkah or another celebration.

LUCKY CHARM
Gift Tag

As the year draws to a close, I like to wish my loved ones a bit of luck for the coming year. With these little pendants, you have the perfect charm on hand.

YOU WILL NEED:

- Modeling clay
- Parchment paper
- ⅛" (3mm) square wooden sticks
- Rolling pin
- Bowl of water
- 1½" (4cm) diameter circle cookie cutter
- Heart-shaped cookie cutter, ½" (1.5cm) high
- Small straw or hollow cake pop stick
- Gold acrylic paint or paint marker
- Paintbrush
- Construction adhesive
- High-gloss clear varnish
- Toothpicks, optional
- Ribbon, string, or twine

1   Roll out the clay on parchment paper with a rolling pin until it is evenly thick. Use the height of the square sticks for reference.

2   Cut out circles from the modeling clay and four hearts per circle.

3   Poke a hole in each of the circles using a straw or cake pop stick. Do not place too close to the edge. Smooth the edges with a finger moistened with water. Leave the pieces to dry, making sure that they do not bend during drying, flipping them over if necessary.

4   Paint all the hearts gold.

5   Glue the hearts onto the cut-out circle using construction adhesive. Arrange in the shape of a clover leaf.

6   Apply a generous amount of high-gloss clear varnish. Make sure that the holes do not become clogged. The holes can be cleaned of varnish using a toothpick. Leave to dry.

7   Attach a ribbon, string, or twine to the charms.

More Ideas

This technique is useful for any design you can think of! As long as you can find a small cookie cutter, then you can make any simple or intricate charm imaginable.

Don't feel limited to cookie cutters for this project. You can make plenty of designs by hand. For example, roll three balls of clay and stack them to make a snowman, add a circle to the clover for a flower, make a circle and spikes for a sun, or shape a simple fruit, such as an apple, strawberry, or lemon.

······· TIP ·······

If you only have a larger heart-shaped
cookie cutter, simply use a larger circle
to ensure they fit.

Acknowledgments

A very special thank-you goes to my family. To my husband, Malte, who has supported this book project so lovingly and appreciatively, and to my children, who patiently put up with my exuberant creativity and at the same time are always a source of inspiration for me. I would also like to thank my siblings, who have so enthusiastically participated in the development of this book.

I would like to dedicate this book to my parents, who gave me the gift of creativity.

About the Author

Daniela Schmidt-Kohl is a mother, social worker and DIY blogger. She lives with her husband and three children on the outskirts of Cologne, right on the Rhine.

On her Instagram account @klickerkram she shares creative creative ideas of all kinds. There you will find inspiration on the topics of DIY, decoration and upcycling for home and garden, as well as original photo projects and impressions from nature. In her creative projects, she uses many different materials, such as modeling clay, wood, paper, concrete, ceramic casting slip and epoxy resin. She is always accompanied by a curiosity for new things - because what could be better than creating things with your own hands?

Index

Note: Page numbers in *italics* indicate projects.

Air Plant Holder, *56–59*
air-hardening clay, 6
Art Deco Relief Gift Tag, *38–41*
Autumn Jewelry Dish, *88–91*
autumn projects, 74–103

Bird Ornament, *18–21*
Boho Chic Wall Mandala, *66–69*
bottle tag, "Fall in Love," *80–83*
bowl of water, 8
box, tiled wooden, *116–19*

candle holder, place card, *124–27*
Christmas Gift Tags, *112–15*
clay
    air-hardening, 6
    modeling, 6
coffee tray, "Milk and Sugar," *76–79*
color
    discolored clay, 114
    grout, 65
    wood, 36
cookie cutters, 8, 9

decoupage options, 46
dishes and trays
    about: checking sizes, 62
    Autumn Jewelry Dish, *88–91*
    Floral Relief Jewelry Dish, *26–29*
    "Milk and Sugar" Coffee Tray, *76–79*
    Tiled Tray, *60–63*

"Fall in Love" Bottle Tag, *80–83*
"Family, Love, Home" Tile Sign, *30–33*
finishes, matte vs. gloss, 68
fish (flying) ornament, *44–47*
Floral Relief Jewelry Dish, *26–29*
flowerpots. *See* plant holders/pots
Flying Fish Ornament, *44–47*
fondant letter stamp, 78
Forever Leaf Ornaments, *84–87*
Framed Plant Print, *92–95*

garland, small plant relief, *48–51*
gift tags. *See* tags and markers
gloss vs. matte finishes, 68
grout color. *See* tiles

herb markers, windowsill, *14–17*
home decor. *See also* dishes and trays; key racks;
    ornaments; wall decor
    Personalized Napkin Rings, *128–31*
    Place Card Candle Holder, *124–27*
    Tiled Wooden Box, *116–19*
    Woodland Plant Stakes, *100–3*
"Home" Key Rack, *34–37*
Houses Key Rack, *106–11*

imprinting textures, 102

Jam Jar Tag, *70–73*
jewelry dishes. *See* dishes and trays

key racks
    "Home" Key Rack, *34–37*
    Houses Key Rack, *106–11*
knife, for cutting clay, 8

leaf ornaments, *84–87*
letter stamp, fondant, 78
Lucky Charm Gift Tags, *136–39*

mandala, wall (boho chic), *66–69*
materials, 6
matte vs. gloss finishes, 68
"Milk and Sugar" Coffee Tray, *76–79*
modeling clay, 6
Modern Circles Wall Decor, *96–99*

napkin rings, personalized, *128–31*
needles/needle tool, 8, 9

ornaments
    Bird Ornament, *18–21*
    Flying Fish Ornament, *44–47*
    Forever Leaf Ornaments, *84–87*
    Simple Star Ornaments, *132–35*
    Winter Ornaments, *120–23*

paintbrushes, 10
parchment paper, 8
Personalized Napkin Rings, *128–31*
Place Card Candle Holder, *124–27*
plant holders/pots
    Air Plant Holder, *56–59*
    Upcycled Tin Can Flowerpot, *22–25*
plant-related items
    about: selecting plants, 50
    Autumn Jewelry Dish, *88–91*
    Christmas Gift Tags, *112–15*
    Forever Leaf Ornaments, *84–87*
    Framed Plant Print, *92–95*
    Small Plant Relief Garland, *48–51*
    Tropical Gift Tag, *52–55*
    Winter Ornaments, *120–23*
    Woodland Plant Stakes, *100–3*
pots. *See* plant holders/pots
pottery tools, 8
projects
    autumn projects, *74–103*
    clay (modeling and air-hardening) for,
      properties, 6
    spring projects, 12–41
    summer projects, 42–73
    tools for, 8–10, 78
    winter projects, 104–139

rolling pins, 8, 9, 10
rubber stamps, 82

sandpaper, 8
Simple Star Ornaments, *132–35*
Small Plant Relief Garland, *48–51*
sponges, 10
spring projects, 12–41

square wooden sticks, 8, 9
stakes for plants, 100–103
stamps, letter, 78
stamps, rubber, 82
star ornaments, *132–35*
straw, small/thin, 8
summer projects, 42–73

tags and markers
    Art Deco Relief Gift Tag, *38–41*
    Christmas Gift Tags, *112–15*
    "Fall in Love" Bottle Tag, *80–83*
    Jam Jar Tag, *70–73*
    Lucky Charm Gift Tags, *136–39*
    Tropical Gift Tag, *52–55*
    Windowsill Herb Markers, *14–17*
tattoos, temporary, crafting with, 54
textures
    imprinting, 102
    rolling on, 24
    tools and improvised tools for, 10
tiles
    about: grout color, 65
    "Family, Love, Home" Tile Sign, *30–33*
    Tiled Tray, *60–65*
    Tiled Wooden Box, *116–19*
tools, supplies, and techniques
    basics, 8–10
    decoupage options, 46
    discolored clay and, 114
    fondant letter stamp, 78
    imprinting textures, 102
    matte vs. gloss finishes, 68
    plant selections, 50
    rolling on textures, 24
    rubber stamps, 82
    temporary tattoos, 54
    wood color, 36
trays. *See* dishes and trays
trimming/modeling tools, 8, 9
Tropical Gift Tag, *52–55*

Upcycled Tin Can Flowerpot, *22–25*

varnishes and paints, 10

wall decor. *See also* key racks
    Boho Chic Wall Mandala, *66–69*
    "Family, Love, Home" Tile Sign, *30–33*
    Framed Plant Print, *92–95*
    Modern Circles Wall Decor, *96–99*
    Small Plant Relief Garland, *48–51*
water bowl, 8
Windowsill Herb Markers, *14–17*
Winter Ornaments, *120–23*
winter projects, *104–139*
wood, color of, 36
wooden box, tiled, *116–19*
Woodland Plant Stakes, *100–3*

Special Thanks

Thank you to Marcia Reiver, PA Guild Master Artisan and ceramics teacher, for reviewing the English edition of this book.

© 2025 by Daniela Schmidt-Kohl

© Christophorus Verlag in der Christian Verlag GmbH, Munich, Germany

Making Pottery without a Kiln is an translation of the 2023 version originally published in German by Christophorus Verlag under the title *Töpfer Dich Glücklich* in Munich, Germany. This version is published by Fox Chapel Publishing Company, Inc.

The patterns contained herein are copyrighted by the author. Readers may make copies of these patterns for personal use. The patterns themselves, however, are not to be duplicated for resale or distribution under any circumstances. Any such copying is a violation of copyright law.

ISBN 978-1-4971-0495-2

Library of Congress Control Number: 2024945968

Shutterstock used: page 6 (mdbildes); page 28 (Aulia1); page 40 (yingko); page 65 (Melandaaini); page 6 (mdbildes); page 28 (Aulia1); page 40 (yingko); page 65 (Melandaaini); pages 72–73 (Wiktoria Matynia); page 94 (Nina Lishchuk); page 94 (Nina Lishchuk); page 138 (Fairy Hollow Photo); page 138 (Fairy Hollow Photo); pages 138–139 (Oleg_Yakovlev).

To learn more about the other great books from Fox Chapel Publishing, or to find a retailer near you, call toll-free 800-457-9112, send mail to 903 Square Street, Mount Joy, PA 17552, or visit us at www.FoxChapelPublishing.com.

We are always looking for talented authors. To submit an idea, please send a brief inquiry to acquisitions@foxchapelpublishing.com.

Printed in the United States of America